香港國際詩歌之夜2013
INTERNATIONAL POETRY NIGHTS IN HONG KONG

I0805471

編輯 Editors

北島 Bei Dao

陳嘉恩 Shelby K. Y. Chan

方梓勳 Gilbert C. F. Fong

柯夏智 Lucas Klein

馬德松 Christopher Mattison

阿多尼斯
Adonis

目錄 Contents

1 بين عينيك وبيني 6
你的眼睛和我之間
Between Your Eyes and Mine

2 الأيام السبعة 9
七日
Seven Days

3 قلت لكم... 12
我對你們說過
I Said unto You

4 وطن 15
祖國
A Homeland

5 أول الشعر 18
詩之初
The Beginning of Poetry

6 ملك الرياح 21
風的君王
King of the Winds

7 إلى سيزيف 25
致西西弗
To Sisyphus

8 أتخيل حبّي 28
我想像我的愛情
I Imagine My Love

9 كيف لي أن أسمّيَ ما بيننا ماضياً؟ 31
我怎麼稱呼我們之間過去的一切？
How Can I Call What Is between Us a Past?

10 ربّما، ليس في الأرض حبٌّ 34
也許，大地上並沒有愛情
Maybe

11 عزف 37
彈奏
Music

12 القصيدة 40
詩篇
To the Poem

13 احتفاءً بالطّفولة 45
紀念童年
Celebrating Childhood

14 دليل للسفر في غابات المعنى 63
在意義叢林旅行的嚮導
Travel Guide to the Forest of Meaning

1 بين عينيك وبيني

حينما أُغرقُ في عينيكِ عيني،
ألمح الفجر العميقا
وأرى الأمس العتيقا
وأرى ما لست أدري،
وأحسّ الكون يجري
بين عينيكِ وبيني.

你的眼睛和我之間

當我把眼睛沉入你的眼睛
我瞥見幽深的黎明
我看到古老的昨天
看到我不能領悟的一切
我感到宇宙正在流動
在你的眼睛和我之間

（薛慶國譯）

Between Your Eyes and Mine

When I drown my eyes in your eyes,
I glimpse the deepest dawning
and see the ancient times;
I see what I do not comprehend
and feel the universe flowing
between your eyes and mine.

(Translated by Kamal Abu Deeb)

2 الأيام السبعة

أيها الأمّ التي تَسخرُ
من حبي ومَقْتي،
أنتِ في سبعة أيام خُلِقْتِ
فخلقتِ الموجَ والأُفْقَ
وريشَ الأغنيهْ
وأنا أيامي السبعةُ جرحٌ وغرابُ
فلماذا الأحْجيَهْ
وأنا مثلُكِ ريحٌ وترابُ؟

七日

你呀，母親，嘲笑我的
愛與恨的母親，
七日之內你被創造，
然後，你創造了波浪和天際，
歌曲的翎羽。
而我，我的七日只是傷口和烏鴉，
為什麼，會留下這個謎？
我和你一樣，也是風，也是泥！

（薛慶國譯）

Seven Days

Mother who mocks
my love and contempt,
you too were made in seven days.
The waves were made then and the horizon,
and the feathers of song,
and my seven days were once wounded and estranged.
Why so unfair then
when I too am made of wind and dust?

(Translated by Khaled Mattawa)

3 قلت لكم...

قلتُ لكم أصغيتُ للبحارْ
تقرأ لي أشعارَها؛ أصغيتْ
للجرَس النائم في المحارْ؛
قلتُ لكم غنّيتْ
في عُرُسِ الشيطان، في وليمة الخُرافهْ؛
قلت لكم رأيتْ
في مطَر التاريخ، في توهّج المسافَهْ
جِنّيّةً وبيتْ؛
لأنني أُبحر في عَينيّ
قلت لكم رأيتُ كلّ شيّ
في الخطْوة الأولى من المسافهْ.

我對你們説過

我對你們説過：我曾傾聽大海
向我朗誦它的詩篇；我曾傾聽
海貝裏面沉睡的搖鈴。
我對你們説過：我曾歌唱
在魔鬼的婚禮上，在神話的宴席上。
我對你們説過：我曾見到
一個精靈，一所殿堂
在歷史的煙雨裏，在距離的燃燒中。
因為我航行在自己的雙眼裏
我對你們説過：一切都在我的眼底，
從旅程的第一步起。

（薛慶國譯）

I Said unto You

I said unto you:
I listened to the seas
reading to me their verses
I listened to the bells
slumbering inside the oyster shells.
I said unto you:
I sang my songs
at Satan's wedding
and the feast of the fable.
I said unto you:
I beheld,
in the rain of history
and the glow of the distance
a fairy and a dwelling.
Because I sail in my eyes,
I said unto you, I beheld
everything
in the first step of the distance.

(Translated by Kamal Abu Deeb)

4 وطن

للوجوهِ التي تَتيبَّسُ تحت قناع الكآبه
أنحني؛ لدروب نسيتُ عليها دموعي
لأبٍ مات أخضراً كالسّحابه
وعلى وجهه شراعُ
أنحني؛ ولطفل يُباعُ
كي يُصلّي وكي يمسحَ الأحذيه —
كلنا في بلادي نصلّي كلنا نمسح الأحذيه
ولِصخرٍ نقشتُ عليه بجوعي
أنّه مَطرٌ يتدحرجُ تحت جفوني وبَرْقُ
ولبيتٍ نقلتُ معي في ضياعيَ تُرابَهْ
أنحني — هذه كلها وَطني، لا دِمشْقُ.

祖國

為那在憂愁的面具下乾枯的臉龐
我折腰；為我忘了為之灑落淚水的小徑
為那像雲彩一樣綠色地死去
臉上還張著風帆的父親
我折腰；為被出賣、
在禱告、在擦皮鞋的孩子
（在我的國家，我們都禱告，都擦皮鞋）
為那塊我忍著饑饉
刻下「它是我眼皮下滾動的雨和閃電」的岩石
為我顛沛失落中把它的土揣在懷裏的家園
我折腰——
所有這一切，才是我的祖國，而不是大馬士革。

（薛慶國譯）

A Homeland

To faces which wither under the mask of melancholy,
I bow.
To roads on which I forgot my tears,
to a father who died as green as a cloud
with a sail upon his face,
I bow.
And to a child who is sold
in order to pray and polish shoes,
(in my country, we all pray and polish shoes),
and to rocks upon which I carved with my hunger
that they were lightning and rain
rolling under my eyelids,
and to a house whose soil I carried in my wanderings,
I bow.
All these are my homeland—
not Damascus.

(Translated by Kamal Abu Deeb)

5 أول الشعر

أجمل ما تكونُ أن تُخلخلَ المدى
والآخرون – بعضهم يظنّك النّداءَ
بعضهم يظنّك الصّدى.
أجمل ما تكونُ أن تكون حجّةً
للنور والظّلام
يكون فيك آخِرُ الكلامِ أوّلَ الكلامِ
والآخرون – بعضهم يرى إليك زَبدًا
وبعضهم يرى إليك خالقًا.
أجمل ما تكون أن تكون هدفًا–
مفترقًا
للصّمتِ والكلامِ.

詩之初

你最美的事，是動搖天地
別人呢，有人以為你不過是回聲
有人卻認定你呼風喚雨
你最美的事，是成為辯辭
被光明和黑暗引以為據
於是，你最後的話語也就是最初的話語
別人呢，有人以為你不過是水泡
有人卻認定你開宗立道
你最美的事，是成為目標
成為分水嶺
區分沉默和話語

（薛慶國譯）

The Beginning of Poetry

The best thing one can be is a horizon.
And the others?
Some will think you are the call
others will think you are its echo.
The best thing one can be is an alibi
for light and darkness
where the last words are your first.
And the others?
Some will see you as the foam of creation
others will think you the creator.
The best thing one can be is a target—
a crossroad
between silence and words.

(Translated by Khaled Mattawa)

6 ملك الرياح

طَرَفٌ رايتي لا تُؤاخي ولا تتلاقى
طَرَفٌ أغنياتي.
ها أنا أحشد الزهور وأستنفر الشجَرْ
وأمدُّ السماء رواقاً
وأحب وأحيا وأُولَدُ في كلِماتي
ها أنا أجمع الفَراشات تحت لواء الصباح
وأربّي الثمارْ
وأبيت أنا والمطَرْ
في الغيوم وأجراسِها، في البحارْ؛
ها أنا أُشرع النجومَ وأُرْسي
وأُنصّبُ نفسي
مَلِكاً للرياح.

風的君王

我的旗幟列成一隊，相互沒有糾纏，
我的歌聲列成一隊。
我正集合鮮花，動員松柏，
把天空鋪展為華蓋。
我愛，我生活，
我在詞語裏誕生，
在早晨的旌旗下召集蝴蝶，
培育果實；
我和雨滴
在雲朵和它的搖鈴裏、在海洋過夜。
我向星辰下令，我停泊矚望，
我讓自己登基，
做風的君王。

（薛慶國譯）

King of the Winds

My banner is an end.
It neither fraternizes
nor meets half-way.
An end are my songs.
Here I am,
amassing the flowers,
alerting the trees,
erecting the sky as a colonnade,
loving, living and getting born
in my words.
Here I am,
gathering the butterflies
under the morning's banner,
nurturing the fruits,
and dwelling with rain
in the clouds and their bells,
in the seas.
Here I am,
sailing the stars
and anchoring them,

and crowning myself
king of the winds.

(Translated by Kamal Abu Deeb)

7 إلى سيزيف

أقسَمْتُ أن أكتبَ فوق الماءْ
أقسمتُ أن أحمل مع سيزيفْ
صخرتَه الصمّاءْ.
أقسمتُ أن أظلّ مع سيزيفْ
أخضعُ لِلحُمّى وللشرارْ
أبحثُ في المحاجر الضريره
عن ريشةٍ أخيره
تكتبُ للعشب وللخريفْ
قصيدةَ الغبارْ

أقسمتُ أن أعيش مع سيزيف.

致西西弗

我發誓在水上書寫
我發誓為西西弗分擔
那塊沉默的山岩
我發誓始終和西西弗一起
經受高熱和火花的炙烤
我要在失明的眼眶裏
尋找最後的羽毛
對著青草、對著秋天
書寫灰塵的詩稿

我發誓要和西西弗同在。

（薛慶國譯）

To Sisyphus

I vowed to write upon water,
I vowed to bear with Sisyphus
his speechless rock.
I vowed to stay with Sisyphus
suffering the fevers and the sparks,
and seeking in blind eyes
a last plume
that writes for autumn and grass
the poem of dust.

I vowed to live with Sisyphus.

(Translated by Kamal Abu Deeb)

8 أتخيل حبّي

أتخيل حبّي:
يتنفس من رئة الشـيء
يأتي إلى
الشّعر في
وَرْدةٍ أو غُبارْ،

يتهامس مع كل شـيء
ويـهمس للكون أحوالهُ
مثلما تفعل الريحُ والشمسُ،
حين تشقاّن صَدْرَ الطبيعة،
أو تسكبان على دفتر الأرض،
حبرَ النهارْ.

我想像我的愛情

我想像我的愛情：
從一樣東西的肺裏吐出
來到
詩歌裏
化身為一朵玫瑰或一粒纖塵

它對著一切傾訴
向宇宙低語它的境遇
就像風兒和太陽
穿破大自然的胸膛
或是，往大地的簿冊
潑上白晝的墨汁

（薛慶國譯）

I Imagine My Love

I imagine my love
breathing with the lungs of all things
and it reaches me
as poetry
of roses or dust
speaks softly to everything
and whispers its news to the universe
the way the wind and sun do
when they split nature's breast
or pour the ink of day
on the earth's book

(Translated by Khaled Mattawa)

9 كيف لي أن أسمّيَ ما بيننا ماضياً؟

كيف لي أن أسمّيَ ما بيننا ماضياً؟
((ليس ما بيننا قصةً،
ليس تُفاَّحَ إنسٍ وجنٍّ
أو دليلاً إلى موسمٍ،
أو مكانْ
ليس شيئاً يؤَرَّخُ)): هذا
ما تقول تصاريفُ أحشائنا.

كيف لي أن أقول، إذاً، حبُّنا
أخذته إليها تجاعيدُ هذا الزمان؟

我怎麼稱呼我們之間過去的一切？

我怎麼稱呼我們之間過去的一切？
「我們之間的不是故事
不是人類或精靈的蘋果
不是引往一個季節
或是一個地方的嚮導
不是可以寫成歷史的事物。」
發自我們肺腑的滄桑如是說。

那麼，我該如何形容我們的愛情
被這個時代的皺紋收納的愛情？

（薛慶國譯）

How Can I Call What Is between Us a Past?

How can I call what is between us a past?
"What is between us is not a story
not a human apple or a jinn's
not a sign of a season
or a place
not anything that could be historicized"
This is what the vicissitudes inside us say

How can I say then that our love
has been taken by the wrinkled hands of time

(Translated by Khaled Mattawa)

10 ربّما، ليس في الأرض حبٌّ

ربّما، ليس في الأرض حبٌّ
غيرُ هذا الذي نتخيل أنّا
سنحظى بهِ، ذات يومٍ.

لا تَقِفْ
تابعِ الرقصَ يا أيها الحب، يا أيها الشعر،
حتى ولو كان موتاً.

也許，大地上並沒有愛情

也許，
大地上並沒有愛情
除了我們幻想著
以為有一天能夠得到的東西

別停下
繼續歡舞，愛情啊，詩歌啊！
哪怕這舞蹈就是死亡。

（薛慶國譯）

Maybe

Maybe
there is no love on earth
except the one we imagine
we will win some day

Don't stop
Go on with the dance, dear love, dear poetry
even if it were death

(Translated by Khaled Mattawa)

11 عزف

لا شيء لا شيء–ريح خفيفة تعزف على قيثار الشجر.
لا شيء، لا شيء.
فراغ، هيهات للكلام أن يملأه.

واحلمْ، احلمْ
ليس الحلم إلا حقيقة في سنّ الرضاعة.
واسأل نفسك، ولا تسألني
ليس هناك أفق مسدود إلا في عقلك.
لكن، من المؤكد تقريباً
أن القصيدة تنهض سحرياً كمثل بيت يتدلى في الفضاء.

يسكن هذا البيت مهاجر اسمه المعنى.

彈奏

沒有什麼，沒有什麼，
是微風在彈奏樹木的吉他；
沒有什麼，沒有什麼，
是話語無法填滿的空虛。

夢想吧，夢想吧，
夢想不過是處於哺乳期的真相。
問你自己，不要問我，
死路，只存在於你的大腦。
然而，幾乎可以肯定：
詩歌神奇地挺起，如同自空中垂下的屋宇。

在這屋宇裏，居住著一位名叫「意義」的遷徙者。

（薛慶國譯）

Music

Nothing, nothing
—a light wind plays the trees' guitars.
Nothing, nothing.
Emptiness. No way for words to fill it.

And I dream, dream
and the dream is nothing but reality in its infancy.
So ask yourself then, don't ask me—
There is no blockade against the horizon except in your mind.
But, it is almost certain
that a poem rises magically like a house dangling from the sky.

In this house an immigrant lives and his name is meaning.

(Translated by Khaled Mattawa)

12 القصيدة

أَلَنْ تغيّري هذا الثّوب الأسود الطويل الذي تلبسينه، حين تجيئين إليّ، أيّتها القصيدة؟ ولماذا يطيب لك أن أضع في كل كلمة منك جزءاً من اللّيل؟ ومن أين لك هذا الدويّ الذي يشقّ الفضاء وأنت بضعة حروف تتناثر على ورقة؟

لا الشيخوخة اليوم، بل الطفولة هي التي تملأ وجهك بالتجاعيد.

أنظري، الآن، كيف يضع النّهار رأسه على كتف الشّمس، بعد أن نام مُنهكاً فيك بين فخذي اللّيل.

وكانت قد وصلت تلك العربة التي تنقل إليك رسائل كتبها الغيب.

قولي للريح، أيّتها القصيدة لن يمنعك أحد من أن تدخلي تحت ثيابي أنَّى شئت ومتى شئت. لكن اسأليها: أيّتها الرّيح، ما مهنتك، ولمن تعملين؟

الفرح والحزن قطرتا ندى على جبينك، والحياة بستان تتنزّه فيه الفصول.

لم أشهد حرباً بين الضّوء والضّوء كمثل الحرب التي اشتعلت بينك وبين سرّة تلك المرأة التي أحببتها في سنوات الطفولة.

أتذكر، فيما كنت أواكب هذه الحرب، أنني قلت للزّمن: لو

كانت لك أذنان، لكنت أرتجل الكون، موسوساً: لا أول إلاّ الآخر.

ألن تغيّري هذا الثّوب الأسود الطويل، أيّتها القصيدة؟

詩篇

詩篇啊，當你造訪我的時候，你不能換掉身上的這件黑色長衫嗎？為什麼，你樂意讓我在你的每個字眼裏，都摻入黑夜的一部分？你不過是一頁紙上散落的幾行文字，可你的回聲，怎麼竟能劈天裂雲？
如今，不是暮年，而是童年，讓你的面孔佈滿皺紋
看哪，此刻，在你那裏，白晝如何將它的頭顱搭在太陽的肩頭；而之前，它曾精疲力盡地在你那裏、在黑夜的兩腿之間入睡。
為你傳遞幽冥書寫的信件的輦車，已經抵達。
詩篇啊，去告訴風：「沒有誰阻攔你鑽進我的衣裳，無論何時，去往任何地方。」但請你向它提問：「風啊，你的職業是什麼？你在為誰勞作？」
歡樂與憂傷是你額頭的兩滴露水，生活是季節徜徉其中的花園。
我從未見過一場光與光之間的戰爭，有如我童年時愛上的那位女士的肚臍眼和你之間的戰爭那麼激烈！
當我追蹤這場戰爭的時候，我想起自己曾對時光說過：「如果你長了兩隻耳朵，那我就會對著宇宙耳語：一切初始都不過是終結。」
詩篇啊，你不能換掉身穿的這件黑色長衫嗎？

（薛慶國譯）

To the Poem

Will you not change the black dress you wear when you come to me?
Why do you insist that I place a piece of night in every word of you? How and where did you acquire this droning power that penetrates space when you are only a few letters on a piece of paper?

It's not old age, but childhood that fills your face with wrinkles.

Look at how the day rests its head on the shoulder of the sun, and how in your company I fall asleep fatigued between the thighs of night.

The cart has arrived, the one that brings the letters of the unknown to you.

Tell the wind nothing will bar you from slipping under my clothes. But do ask the wind, "What kind of work do you do, and who do you work for?"

Happiness and sadness are two drops of dew on your forehead, and life is an orchard where the seasons stroll.

I have never seen a war between two lights like the one that erupted between you and the navel of a woman I loved in childhood.

Do you remember how I followed that war? And how once I turned to time and said,
"If you had two ears to listen with
you too would have walked the universe, deluded and disheveled,
no beginning to your end."

Will you ever change the black dress you wear when you come to me?

(Translated by Khaled Mattawa)

13 احتفاءً بالطّفولة

تتمنّى الرّيح نفسها
أن تتحوّل إلى عَربةٍ
تجرُّها الفراشات.

أتذكَّر الجنون –
يَتّكىء، للمرة الأولى، على وسادةِ العقل :
كنتُ أحاوِرُ جسَدي.

كان جسدي فكرةً
أكتبُها باللّون الأحمر، –
(كان الأحمر أجملَ كرسيّ للشمس
وكانت الألوان كلّها
تصلّي فوق بساطٍ أحمر)

اللّيلُ نفسُه
قنديلٌ آخر.

في كلّ غصن ذراعُ :

رسالةٌ يحملها الفضاء
ويؤكِّدها جسدُ الرّيح.

تُصرّ الشّمسُ، في هذه الآونة،
أن تلبسَ الضّباب
حين تلاقيني :
أهو عتابُ الضّوء؟

يا لأَيّامي الماضية، –
كانت تسير في نومها
وكنتُ أتوكّأ عليها.

الحبُّ والحلم قوسان
أضع بينهما جسدي
وبه أتعرّف على العالم.

كثيراً،
رأيتُ الهواء يطير بقدمين من العُشب

والطريقَ ترقص بقدمين من الهواء.

رغباتي ورودٌ
تتبقَّع بها أيامي.

جُرحتُ باكرًا،
وباكرًا عرفت:
الجراحُ هي التي خلقتني.

لا أزال أسير وراء الطفل
الذي لا يزال يسيرُ في أعضائي،–
الآن يقف على ذروة سلّمٍ من الضوء،
يبحث عن زاويةٍ يستريح فيها
لكن، لكي يقرأ من جديدٍ وجه الليل.

لو كان القمرُ بيتاً
لرفضت خطواتي أن تطأ عتبته،–
مأخوذٌ بهذا الغبار

الذي يحمله إليّ هواء الفصول.

أمشي،–
أضع يداً في الهواء
وأضع يدي الثانية في جدائلَ أتخيّلها.

النّجمةُ هي كذلك
حصاةٌ في حَقْل الفلك.

وحده الذي امتزَج بالأفق
يقدر أن يفتح طريقاً.

...قَمرٌ،– شيخٌ
كرسيّه الليل، وعكّازه الضوء.

ماذا أقول لجسدي الآخر
الذي تركته بين أنقاض البيت
الذي وُلدتُ فيه؟

كلا، لا يقدر أن يروي طفولتي
إلا تلك النّجوم التي تتلألأ فوقه
وتُبقّع بخطواتها دروبَ المساء

لا تزالُ طفولتي
تولد بين يدي ضوءٍ أجهل اسمه
وهو الذي يسمّيني.

ذلك النهر،– كان يصنع منه مرآة
ليسألها عن أحزانه،
وكان يصنع من أحزانه مطراً
لكي يقلّد الغيوم.

قريةٌ صغيرةٌ هي طفولتك
مع ذلك،
لن تقطعَ تُخومَها
مهما أوغلتَ في السفر.

أيّامه بحيراتٌ
وذكرياته أجسادٌ عائمة.

أنت الهابطُ من الأعالي
في جبالِ الماضي،
كيف تقدر أن تصعد إليها ثانيةً،
ولماذا؟

زمنٌ – بابٌ مغلق
لا أقدر، لا أقدر أن أفتحه.
سحري متعب
وتعاويذي نائمة.

ولدتُ في قريةٍ
صغيرةٍ وسرّيةٍ كأنها الرَّحِم
ولم أخرج منها أبداً،–
حبّي للمحيطِ لا للشّواطئ.

紀念童年

就連風兒，
也希望化為
蝴蝶牽引的輦車。

我憶起：當瘋狂
第一次倚靠理智的枕墊時，
我正和我的身體對話。

我的身體曾是一個思想，
我用紅色書寫；
紅，是太陽最美的座椅，
所有的色彩，
都跪倒在一塊紅毯上祈禱。

黑夜本身
也是一盞燈。

每一棵樹枝上都長著翅膀：
那是太空攜帶的信箋，
風的身體為之作證。

此刻，在迎接我的時候，
固執的太陽
非要披上霧靄的衣裳
——這是對光的責難嗎？

我往昔的日子啊：
你在睡眠中行進，
而我正倚靠著你的身體。

愛與夢是括弧的兩端，
我把我的身體置於中間，
以此，我認識世界。

經常，
我見到空氣用青草的雙腳飛翔，
我見到道路用空氣的雙腳起舞。

我的願望是玫瑰，
點綴著我的歲月。

我自幼便受過傷，

我自幼就懂得：
是傷口將我創造。

我依然追隨著那個兒童，
他依然在我的身體內行走；
現在，他站在光之梯的頂端，
尋找一個小憩的角落，
不過，那是為了重讀黑夜的臉龐。

如果月亮是一間房屋，
我的腳步會拒絕踩踏它的門檻：
月亮正在沉迷於
季節之風給我攜來的塵土。

我行走，
我的一隻手垂在空氣中，
另一隻手插入我想像的髮辮。

一顆星星，
也是太空原野裏的一粒石子。

只有和天際融合成一體，
才能開闢一條道路。

月亮：一個老翁，
他的座椅是夜晚，月光是他的拄杖。

我該對我的另一個身體説些什麼？
——我把它遺留在
我出生的老宅的廢墟間。
不，只有在天空閃亮的星星，
只有用腳步點綴黃昏之路的星星，
才能敍述我的童年。

我的童年依然在降生，
在一束我不知其名的光的面前，
一束為我命名的光的面前。

這條河，他用河做成一面鏡子，
以便對著鏡子詢問他的憂傷；
他用憂傷做成雨水，
以便仿效雲彩的模樣。

你的童年是小村莊，
可是，
你走不出它的邊際，
無論你遠行到何方。

他的日子是湖泊，
他的記憶是漂浮的身體。

你從往昔之山的高峰降下，
你怎麼能，你為什麼
要再次登上山峰？

時光：一扇緊閉的門，
我不能，不能打開這扇門。
我的幻術疲憊了，
我的符咒已經入睡。

我出生於一個村莊，
一個像子宮一樣，隱秘的小村莊。

我從沒有走出那裏：
我愛的不是岸陸，我的愛屬於海洋。

（薛慶國譯）

Celebrating Childhood

Even the wind wants
to become a cart
pulled by butterflies.

I remember madness
leaning for the first time
on the mind's pillow.
I was talking to my body then.

My body was an idea
I wrote in red.
Red is the sun's most beautiful throne
and all the other colors
worship on red rugs.

Night is another candle.

In every branch, an arm,
a message carried in space
echoed by the body of the wind.

The sun insists on dressing itself in fog
when it meets me:
Am I being scolded by the light?

Oh, my past days—
they used to walk in their sleep
and I used to lean on them.

Love and dreams are two parentheses.
Between them I place my body
and discover the world.

Many times
I saw the air fly with two grass feet
and the road dance with feet made of air.

My wishes are flowers
staining my days.

I was wounded early,
and early I learned

that wounds made me.

I still follow the child
who still walks inside me.
Now he stands at a staircase made of light
searching for a corner to rest in
and to read the face of night again.

If the moon were a house,
my feet would refuse to touch its doorstep.
They are taken by dust
carrying me to the air of seasons.

I walk,
one hand in the air,
the other caressing tresses
that I imagine.

A star is also
a pebble in the field of space.

He alone
who is joined to the horizon
can build new roads.

A moon, an old man,
his seat is night
and light is his walking stick.

What shall I say to the body I abandoned
in the rubble of the house
in which I was born?
No one can narrate my childhood
except those stars that flicker above it
and that leave footprints
on the evening's path.

My childhood is still
being born in the palms of a light
whose name I do not know
and who names me.

Out of that river he made a mirror
and asked it about his sorrow.
He made rain out of his grief
and imitated the clouds.

Your childhood is a village.
You will never cross its boundaries
no matter how far you go.

His days are lakes,
his memories floating bodies.

You who are descending
from the mountains of the past,
how can you climb them again,
and why?

Time is a door
I cannot open.
My magic is worn,
my chants asleep.

I was born in a village,
small and secretive like a womb.
I never left it.
I love the ocean not the shores.

(Translated by Khaled Mattawa)

14 دليل للسفر في غابات المعنى

ما الشعر؟
سفنٌ تبحرُ ولا مرافئَ لها.

ما الخيال؟
عطرُ الواقع.

ما الوجه؟
أقربُ مرفأٍ لهجرة الدمع.

ما النهار؟
أوسعُ قفصٍ لأشعّة الشّمس.

ما الوردة؟
رأسٌ يربّى للقطع.

ما الغبار؟
زفيرٌ يتصاعدُ من رئةِ
الأرض.

ما المطر؟
آخر مسافرٍ
ينزلُ من قطار الغيم.

ما القلق؟
غضونٌ
وتجاعيدُ
في حرير الشرايين.

ما الزمن؟
ثوبٌ نلبسهُ
ولا نقدرُ أن نخلعه.

ما الفقر؟
قبرٌ متحركٌ فوق الأرض.

在意義叢林旅行的嚮導

什麼是詩歌？
遠航的船隻
沒有碼頭。

什麼是幻想？
現實的香氣。

什麼是臉龐？
眼淚遷徙
途經的最近港灣。

什麼是白晝？
囚禁陽光的最大的籠子。

什麼是貧窮？
在大地上移動的墳墓。

什麼是玫瑰？
為了被斬首而生長的頭顱。

什麼是塵土？

從大地之肺發出的一聲嘆息。

什麼是雨？
從烏雲的列車上，下來的最後一位旅客。

什麼是焦慮？
褶子和皺紋，在神經的絲綢上。

什麼是時光？
我們穿上的衣服，卻再也脫不下來。

（薛慶國譯）

Travel Guide to the Forest of Meaning

What is poetry?
Vessel headed for no port.

What is imagination?
The scent of reality.

What is the face?
Port for the migration of tears.

What is day?
A cage to trap sunlight.

What is poverty?
A grave moving above ground.

What is rose?
A head which grows in order to be cut off.

What is dust?
A sigh which comes from the lung of the earth.

What is rain?
The last passenger to come off the train of cloud.

What is anxiety?
Creases and wrinkles on the silk of the nerves.

What is time?
Clothes which once put on we cannot take off.

(Translated by Zhang Jian)

阿多尼斯，原名阿里・艾哈邁德・賽義德・伊斯伯爾，1930年出生於敘利亞北部農村。他畢業於大馬士革大學哲學系，並在貝魯特聖約瑟大學獲文學博士。

阿多尼斯迄今共創作了50多部著作，包括詩集、文學與文化評論、散文、譯著等。阿多尼斯不僅是當今阿拉伯世界最重要的詩人、思想家、文學理論家，也在世界詩壇享有盛譽。評論家認為，阿多尼斯對阿拉伯詩歌的影響，可以同龐德或艾略特對英語詩歌的影響相提並論。阿多尼斯對阿拉伯政治、社會與文化的深刻反思和激烈批判，也在阿拉伯文化界引發爭議，並產生廣泛影響。

阿多尼斯曾屢獲各種國際文學大獎，如匹茲堡國際詩歌論壇獎(1971)、黎巴嫩國家詩歌獎(1974)、布魯塞爾詩歌雙年展大獎(1986)、法國讓・馬里奧外國文學獎(1991)、地中海獎(1994)、土耳其希克梅特文學獎(1994)、意大利Lerici-Pea獎(2000)、阿聯酋阿維斯文化基金獎(2004)、挪威比昂松獎(2007)、中國中坤國際詩歌獎(2009)、德國歌德文學獎(2011)等。1997年，法國政府授予阿多尼斯文學藝術騎士勳章。

Ali Ahmad Said Esber, known to readers as **Adonis**, was born in a rural village in Syria in 1930. He graduated with a degree in philosophy from the Damascus University and went on to earn a doctoral degree in Arabic literature from St. Joseph University in Beirut.

Adonis has written more than fifty books of poetry, criticism, essays, and translation in his native Arabic. He is recognized as one of the most important poets and theorists of literature in the Arab world, and one of the most important contemporary poets and thinkers in any language or context. His influence on Arabic poetry can be compared with that of Pound or Eliot on poetry in English, combined, however, with a radical and secular critique of his society.

Adonis's many awards include the International Poetry Forum Award (Pittsburgh, 1971), National Poetry Prize (Lebanon, 1974), Grand Prix des Biennales Internationales de la Poésie (Belgium, 1986), Prix de Poésie Jean Malrieu Étranger (France, 1991), Prix de la Méditerranée (France, 1994), Nazim Hikmet Prize (Turkey, 1994), Lerici-Pea Prize (Italy, 2000), Oweiss Cultural Prize (UAE, 2004), BjØrnson Prize (Norway, 2007), Zhong Kun International Poetry Prize (China, 2009), and Goethe Literature Prize (Germany, 2011). In 1997 the French government named him Commandeur de l'Ordre des Arts et des Lettres.

出版 Publisher
香港中文大學出版社 The Chinese University Press

封面影像 Cover Image
北島 Bei Dao

出版日期 Date of Publication
二零一三年十一月 November 2013

國際書號 ISBN
978-962-996-610-2

本書版權為香港中文大學所有，個別詩篇及翻譯的版權則屬個別作者及譯者所有。除獲本大學書面允許外，不得在任何地區，以任何方式，任何文字翻印、仿製或轉載本書文字或圖像。

This collection and editorial matters © The Chinese University of Hong Kong, 2013
Individual poems and translations © Individual contributors
All rights reserved. No part of this book may be reproduced or transmitted by any means without written permission from The Chinese University of Hong Kong.

香港國際詩歌之夜 2013 International Poetry Nights in Hong Kong 2013
主辦單位 Organizers
香港中文大學文學院 Faculty of Arts, The Chinese University of Hong Kong
香港浸會大學文學院 Faculty of Arts, Hong Kong Baptist University
香港科技大學人文社會科學學院 School of Humanities and Social Science, The Hong Kong University of Science and Technology

合作夥伴 In Partnership With
英國文化協會 British Council

協辦單位 Co-organizers
時刻文化 Moment Communications
香港中文大學出版社 The Chinese University Press

贊助 Sponsors
香港兆基創意書院 HKICC Lee Shau Kee School of Creativity
中國會 The China Club
周凱旋基金會 Chau Hoi Shuen Foundation

Printed in Hong Kong